Love Thoughts From Crumpled Pages

What am I even doing?

J. Sawyer

BookLeaf Publishing

India | USA | UK

Made with ❤ on the BookLeaf Publishing Platform
www.bookleafpub.in
www.bookleafpub.com

Dedication

To those who continue to cheer me on (in public and in
private).
To those who broke my heart into pieces.
To me.

With my deepest appreciation, thank you.

Preface

This collection of poems, thoughts, and ramblings has been sown together from notes, journals, crumpled pieces of paper, and 3am dreams. I am still working on loving all of me. I am still in search of my forever. Maybe one day, we will meet.

Acknowledgements

I would like to acknowledge the sun for reminding me you can never shine too bright, the moon for reminding me to stay consistent and show up, and the water for bringing calm and clarity to any problem I have.

1. The Shutdown

"You never realize your light went out, until you look
back and all you see is darkness." Me

"It didn't happen that way."

"You are being overdramatic."

"That never happened."

"That's not how I said it."

"That's not what I meant."

"It doesn't have to be that deep."

"Why would you think that way??

The response comes, my body gets hot, my throat closes,
my chest pinches, pins and needles shoot through my
fingers and toes, silence takes over, and all in an instant,

the shutdown occurs.

Shame and embarrassment stifle any knowing that might be true. The shrink happens a quarter millimeter at a time so no one notices you disappearing. Stay in your place, your perspective is not relevant here.

2. Lies

"Half a truth is often a great lie." Benjamin Franklin

The snake of lies always comes at night.
When I am at my most vulnerable.
It is there, my brain allows the truth to get
overshadowed.
It is there, new stories with characters unseen, are
brought to life.
It is there, I question what is real and what is fake.
It is there, my worth is questioned.
It is there, the timeline of my life gets twisted. It is there,
my worst fears come to life.

Then, the sun rises and the snake slithers away to hide in
the corners of my sheets.
Only to wait for me, when darkness comes again.

3. Lost

"Now you're lost, lost in the heat of it all." - Frank Ocean

What would you say if you could?
She replied: "I'm just looking for you to see it and get it.
In case you didn't know, it was for you.
But if you didn't get it, I guess I got my answer."
Anything else?

"Yes", she replied. "I'll get over it. I just didn't want to
have to."

4. Death of Love

"Don't break your own heart trying to fill someone else's." Bianca Sparacino

We cannot grow where we were not meant to be.
We will wither.
We will shrink.
Our eyes will grow dark.
Our skin will become sticky.
Our mouths will feel dry.
Others will water us, but our dreams, motivations, and
hopes will continue to fall flat.
We cannot grow where we were not meant to be.
So why do we stay so long?

5. Faith

"So we live by faith and not sight." 2 Corinthians 5:7

Fluff walked ahead just enough to feel his independence.
Her confidence in his was steady and strong - no
questions.
She never questioned the beautiful outcomes created by
Him, yet sat in worry during the wait.
Confidence feels beautiful and light, questioning feels
heavy and scary.
What do you need to do to get to the beautiful and light?
And why is it so scary?

6. Space

"The right one does not stand in your way. They make space for you to step forward." Rupi Kaur

What would it look like to take up space?
How do you walk into spaces in which you don't feel
included, wanted or enough to be in?
What would it look like if you just didn't care?
If you held your head high and took up space.
We are all terrified inside - 'What if I'm not enough?
What if they laugh at me? What if I say something
stupid? What if I offend someone?'
The real truth is, no one cares.
Most of us are living life terrified.
Most of us are so wrapped up in ourselves, we aren't
really seeing others clearly.
Most of us have no idea what we are doing, but we just
keep showing up.
Walking with our head held high, pretending we know
what we are doing.
If you knew you had nothing to lose, how would you

take up space?
How would you move differently?

7. Sun and Moon

"You never know when a moment and a few sincere words, can have an impact on a life." Zig Ziglar

I want the story with you - said the Sun to the Moon.
Remember the walk that changed us.
The laughter that couldn't hide.
When I poured my light onto the water, to allow your words.

Yes whispered the Moon, *when I cast shadows to allow for the kiss that brought you to tears.*
Your hand in mine.

The Sun beamed - *your rain quenched my thirst.*
I can't move.

The Moon glowed full - *I'm terrified but alive.*
I don't want to ask you, yet I do.
The romantic comedy plays in my head.

The Sun glimmered - *our first date.*
The paper on the table.
The giggles.

The Moon stuttered - *but I don't want to ruin what we have.*
It's just...you feel like home.
And I don't want to stop.
But maybe.
Someday.
What if.

The Sun whispered - *I don't want to say it.*
It could be the beginning.
Or could be the end.
Does it have to be either?

The Moon quietly whispered, as she took her form as new.

8. Attached

"It takes two flints to make a fire." Louisa May Alcott

I want a teammate.
Just the two of us - a song of ours.
In sink - with our eyes.
Working through the shit - feeling it with our hands.
I want a teammate.
So far I've found not much.

Still looking.

I got you.
I need you.
I hear you.
Fall back.
Let's pray.
Let's talk.
Let's breathe.
Meet my...
Know my...

Believe my...
Understand my...
You are my...

Teammate.

Yet.

I'm still waiting.
Are you out there?

9. Maybe for Real

'"Maybe this time, like every time, it is about me." Me

Do you think we need time - YES.
I'm hoping this is mutual.
Because I'm the girl that will go through it with you - but
I can't sit on the sidelines waiting to be called in.
I'm the wife.
I'm the forever.
I'm the girl.
And yet, I keep playing the side kick.
Because deep down, I still don't think I'm worth it.

Damn that stings.

Was I the place holder for the girl you will do forever
with?

We will see.

10. Was It Love?

*"Love is when you meet someone who tells you
something new about yourself." Andre Breton*

I never knew you, then suddenly I did.
And it was nothing more than a slow burn with you.
I am scared because.
But also not, because
I just trust you.
I love you.
I am so here for whatever this is.
Are you with me?
Or am I to stand alone, in this puddle of feelings?

11. At First

"You had me at hello." Jerry Maguire

It was electric.
It was sunshine.
It was light.
I was sure.
I felt you, even when I wasn't near you.
Your eyes told a story.
Your hand reassured me, your embrace created safety.
But then.
When.
I don't even know when it happened.
It was over.

12. Quiet Love

"And over all these virtues put on love, which binds them all together in perfect unity." Colossians 3:14

I barely heard you come in.
It felt like floating - freeing and calm.
Breathing with the waves of your heartbeat.
Hearing the echoes of pillow talk in my ears.
The comfort of my bed, imprints I know will be there,
sheets fresh from the dryer.
Falling in effortlessly after a long day, the security of
knowing.
The warmth of someone's arms, wrapped tightly around
me, wanting nothing more than to hold me.

Quiet love is fearless.
Quiet love is one everyone can feel, but not many can
see.
Quiet love is the welcoming sun, after a torrential storm.
Quiet love is the smell of grass, after a long cold winter.
Quiet love is the fresh blanket of snow, to start again.

Quiet love is given without being asked or chased or
begged for.
Quiet love shows up.

13. I Want

"Find someone you can heal with." Young Pueblo

To save you a seat.
To hug and kiss your face when I see you.
To say 'we'.
To plan what our future looks like.
To ask vulnerable questions with reassuring answers.
To know.
To trust.
To be yours.
To laugh at stupid jokes.
To feel safe with you.
To not care what you do.
To know.
To have it be God and Us and Kids.
To read scripture and discuss feelings.
To read and discuss ideas.
To talk.
To be able to say the story in my head.

To not feel... the way I have.

14. To Be Honest

"You have dug your soul out of the dark, you have fought to be here; do not go back to what buried you." Bianca Sparacino

No disrespect.

If I take the time to be vulnerable with you, share my feelings, and come to you -
I have already taken time and overthought everything.

If I share how your actions and words have hurt me -
and you disregard me by somehow stating we are less than.
I will understand my place.

How have I not seen it - hidden in plain sight.

The decision was made, the same way the tide rolls in.

Without any speaking.

Either of us could have left. Yes.

You could have respected me enough to walk away when
you knew you could never give.

No disrespect.

But you are truly disrespectful, to love.

15. Turn Around

"Sometimes we go back and repeat an old mistake just so we can remember why we moved forward." Young Pueblo

Because I was sitting on your couch, standing on your driveway, and waiting in the parking lot, begging.
A tear stained face.
For you to choose me.
For you to put your ego aside and see me.
Want me.
Fight for me.
Reach out for me.
Turn around, because I am here.

Yet, you continue to walk away.

16. One Foot

"Lovers are lunatics" Latin saying

One foot in, one foot out - that is how it's always been.
Your eyes, energy, and heart say maybe, yet you
continue to entertain a circus.
The answer to the questions are always - yet.
So it needs to be a no.
One foot in, one foot out - that is how it's always been.
Love me out loud.
In the shower.
With friends.
With family.
In public.
In pictures.
In energy.
In spirit.
In life.
If we aren't growing together, what are we doing?
If I know I am worth more, why do I keep accepting one
foot out the door?

17. Maybe

"Maybe this time, for the first time. Love won't hurry away. Maybe this time. Maybe this time, I'll win." Maybe
This Time

Made your own rules, I didn't know how to follow.
Answered questions in riddles of actions not matching words, never straight forward.
Yet
Brought me to a place, I thought we could be.
Even though the answer was always going to be, no.

18. Peace

"You cannot love someone into loving you if they do not." Bianca Sparacino

If you can't bring it, keep it, or help me feel it -

Walk away.

19. It Starts

*"Taking a moment to figure out how you really feel
instead of letting old patterns decide for you is one of the
most authentic things you can do." Young Pueblo*

In the aftermath of what had happened,
she decided to walk through the fog into the light.

She decided to trust her gut and welcome the unknown
with open arms.
She decided to step into the world, open eyes, heart, and
soul and use the instrument she was born to use.
Her voice.
It starts with day 1.

20. She Is

"You always find it when you stop looking" - Me.

She was the tornado they needed to rebuild.
She was the sun they never knew they needed.
She was the fire missing from the night,
and the moon to guide them home.
She was the girl you never knew you needed.
She was the missing beat to your heart.
She was her own knight in shining armor, riding her
own horse, determined to bring peace to her life.
And in doing so, she blazed a trail of light, love, and
peace to anyone willing to see it.
Yet - alone, she must be.

To find out who she is.

21. 44 Laps

"Say yes to life, even though you know it may devour you." Stephen Larsen

44 laps around the sun.

Spins in the sea.

How the world looks so different when it's just me.

If it were just me - alone.

Where would I be?

How would I move?

What stops me from moving?

What stops me from leaving?

At the end of the day - does fear hold us all in place?

Why does it take some of us so long to get there and other faster?

What if no one shows up?

What if everyone shows up?

Does that validate me?

Who do I actually want to be?

In the end - it's the people I feel most comfortable with.

The people I see and interact with.

I don't want low vibration.

I don't want the maybe.

I don't want people around me that know nothing about
me.